Bip and the Nut

By Cameron Macintosh

Bip the bug sits on
a big red rug.

He gets a big nut.

Bip taps the nut.

Tap, tap, tap!

Ant is on the big red rug.

Ant gets the nut!

Bip is sad.

Bip can see fig jam.

Bip gets the jam
and runs to Ant.

Ant can see the fig jam!

Ant sips the fig jam.

Bip gets the big nut!

CHECKING FOR MEANING

1. Who had the nut at the start of the story? *(Literal)*

2. Why was Bip sad? *(Literal)*

3. Why did Bip give the fig jam to Ant? *(Inferential)*

EXTENDING VOCABULARY

fig	What is a *fig*? Look at the word. What new word would you make if you took away the *f* and put a *b* at the start?
jam	What are some words you know that describe the taste of *jam*? E.g. sweet, sticky. How many sounds are in the word *jam*? What are they?
red	In this story, which item is *red*? What other things do you know that are *red*? E.g. tomatoes, fire engines, flowers, apples.

MOVING BEYOND THE TEXT

1. What would you do if a friend had something that you wanted?

2. What foods do people often take on picnics?

3. Why do ants often crawl on picnic rugs?

4. If you were Bip, how would you have tried to get the nut back?

SPEED SOUNDS

Dd	Jj	Oo	Gg	Uu

Cc	Bb	Rr	Ee	Ff	Hh	Nn

Mm	Ss	Aa	Pp	Ii	Tt

PRACTICE WORDS

on

big

fig

bug

runs

rug

red

sad

jam

gets

and

nut